TODAY I DID MY VERY
BEST, NOW IT'S TIME TO
PUT MY BRAIN TO REST.

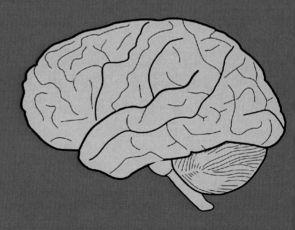

I CLOSE MY EYES WITH LOVE IN MY HEART, TOMORROW IS A NEW START.

I AM LOVED SO DEEPLY,
KNOWING THAT I CAN
SLEEP PEACEFULLY.

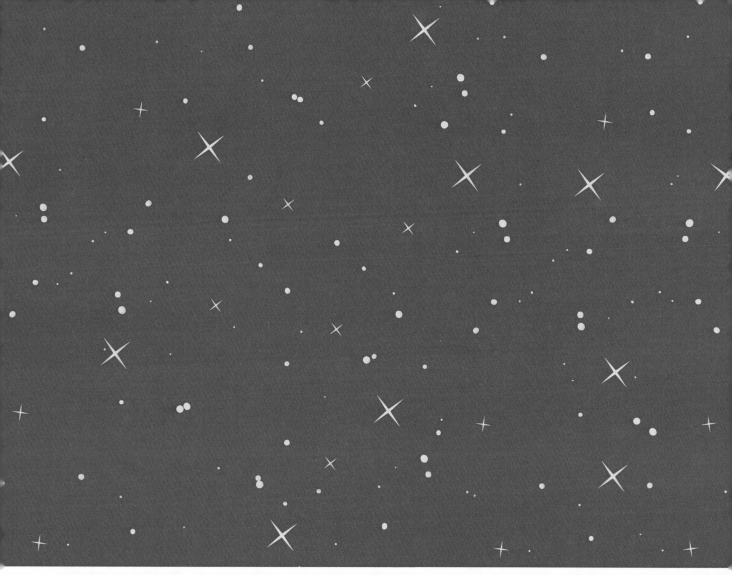

FOUR
4

I BRUSHED MY TEETH AND NOW I AM TUCKED IN, I AM SO EXCITED FOR TOMORROW TO BEGIN .

I GAVE TODAY MY VERY ALL, I NEED A LOT OF GOOD SLEEP TO GROW STRONG AND TALL .

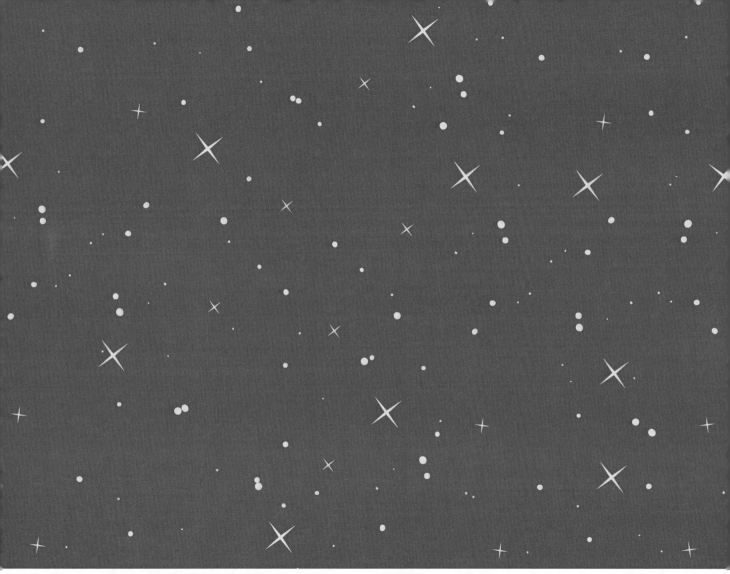

I HAVE THE ABILITY TO TAKE ON TOMORROW AND SUCCEED NO MATTER WHERE THAT PATH MAY LEAD .

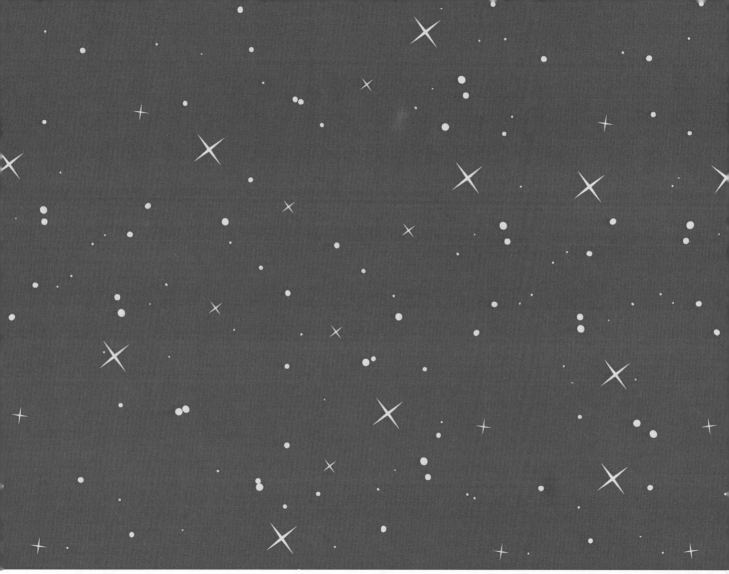

THE MOON AND STARS
ARE SHINING BRIGHT
IT'S TIME FOR ME TO
CALL IT A NIGHT.

EIGHT
8

I PRAY FOR GOOD
DREAMS THROUGHOUT
THE NIGHT I HOPE THE
BED BUGS DON'T BITE.

NINE
9

TODAY I CONQUERED AT LEAST ONE OF MY FEARS, KNOWING THAT MY MIND IS CLEAR.

MY BODY HELPED ME
GET THROUGH THE DAY,
I AM GOING TO SLEEP
NOW TO GIVE IT THANKS.